Accord
New & Selected Poems

JOHN IDRIS JONES

INDEPENDENT INNOVATIVE INTERNATIONAL

Published by Cinnamon Press
Meirion House, Glan yr afon, Tanygrisiau
Blaenau Ffestiniog, Gwynedd, LL41 3SU
www.cinnamonpress.com

ISBN: 978-1-907090-31-8
British Library Cataloguing in Publication Data. A CIP record for this book can be obtained from the British Library.

Designed and typeset in Palatino by Cinnamon Press. Cover design by Jan Fortune-Wood from original artwork, 'vertical view of waterfall in Wales' (Pistyll Rhaeadr, Llanrhaiadr-ym-Mochnant) by Steve Heap © agency dreamstime.com.

Printed in Poland

Cinnamon Press is represented in the UK by Inpress Ltd www.inpressbooks.co.uk and in Wales by the Welsh Books Council www.cllc.org.uk.

Acknowledgements

The poem 'First Day' was included in the AQA examination board GCSE June 2009 English Literature (specification B) Foundation Tier paper. 'Laugharne Castle' was included in *The Students' Book GCSE English/English Literature*, Roger Lane (Oxford U.P.; 2003). 'First Day' and 'Elvis Presley' were included in *Revise WJEC GCSE English Literature*, Roger Lane (Oxford U.P.; 2004).

Various poems were included in the following anthologies: *The Lilting House; an anthology of Anglo-Welsh poetry 1917-67*; eds John Stuart Williams, Meic Stephens, (J.M.Dent; 1969): *Anglo-Welsh Poetry 1480-1980*; eds Raymond Garlick & Roland Mathias, (Poetry Wales Press, 1984): *Axed Between the Ears*; ed David Kitchen; (Heinemann, 1987): *The Third Day, Landscape and the Word*, ed Kathy Miles, (Gomer, 1995): *Say That Again*; eds Mairwen Jones and John Spink, (Gomer, 1997): *Love*; ed Dewi Roberts; (The Corgi Series, Carreg Gwalch, 2002): *Work*; ed Dewi Roberts; (The Corgi Series, Gwasg Carreg Gwalch, 2004): *Poetry 1900-2000*; ed Meic Stephens; (Parthian, Library of Wales, 2007).

Poems have been included in the following periodicals: *Envoi; Poetry Wales; New Welsh Review; Cambria; Roundyhouse*.

Some of these poems were included in the author's previous collection, *Renewals*; (Conybeare Publishing, Cardiff, 1999).

Contents

Foreword

I first came across the work of John Idris Jones in *The Anglo-Welsh Review* in the days when it was edited by Roland Mathias. His poem 'To Ioan Madog, Poet, Ancestor,' made an instant impression on me. It began:

> Grandfather spoke of you
> (As she lay, arthritic, in her bed)
> As a large gay man,
> A blacksmith who shaped hoops
> For ships. Portmadoc built them.
> So many you could dance from deck to deck
> The moil of labour in your ears mixed
> With the rich note of the native tongue.

This was the 1960s, when for most people the word 'gay' had nothing to do with sexual orientation and Portmadoc was not yet Porthmadog. The poem sounded an elegiac note, mourning the passing of a way of life and the people who had nourished it.

John Idris Jones is a Welshman through and through, and not only that but a north Welshman. The distinction is important. He lacks the easy – sometimes deceptively easy – gregariousness of the Welshman of the Valleys. He is reticent, perhaps more cautious than he used to be, but with strong feelings that often find expression in his poetry.

His early experience of America – he graduated at Cornell University and later lectured in Northern Illinois– gave him a taste for the unexpected and a delight in chance encounters. One of the poems arising from these,

'Lawrence, Kansas,' ends with three lines that I find peculiarly haunting:

> And I knew of course that with that yellow-haired girl
> Sitting quietly next to me
> We were all like Mr Ford manufacturers of dreams.

Back home in Wales, he developed an interest in publishing and brought out many fine books under the John Jones imprint - which still exists – before taking up teaching. His retirement has given him more time to devote to his true calling of poetry. He has an unmistakeable voice, a 'speaking' voice with subtle rhythms and echoes not only of the Welsh language he speaks fluently but of the old culture of Wales. There is a sense in his poetry not so much of a past Wales as of a Wales existing parallel with the present, influencing those with the antennae to perceive it. A sampler spotted in a Caernarfon junk shop sets him off on a spiritual journey touching past and future. An empty field inspires thoughts of the great house that once stood there. For him it 'still exists, like history/below ground.'

His most recent poems include celebrations of family life, a tribute to R.S. Thomas, and a vivid recapturing of Pavarotti's visit to Llangollen which tells how at the first note everything around seemed to be 'smothered in a brown amber.' A praise poem to his wife Denise echoes a line by Theodore Roethke:

> I know a woman, lovely in her bones,
> who takes my life as on a cloud
>
> who takes my weight and lightens it
> and takes my breath to ease around herself.

John Idris Jones, who was 70 in March 2008, is above all a poet of place. Wales is his home, Clwyd the hearth where he takes his ease. As a young man in America, he knew it. Offered a professorship in Illinois, he decided to return to Wales. 'Roots predominate,' he observes. One of his best poems is 'Green Country, Clwyd'. It begins:

> Place is important on this globe
> of furrows with troughs of memory
> following our plough. Everywhere
> there are fragments.
> A mound of earth will make a stone, or Caesar.

That's John Idris Jones – ploughing his lonely furrow, conveying subtle truths in simple language. Elsewhere he has written, 'The sky is quiet with distant birds.' Beat that.

Herbert Williams, March 2011

Introduction - The Poetry of John Idris Jones

It was over half a century ago, in 1957, when I was a student at Keele, that I first met him, a black-haired teenager with bright eyes and smiling boyish face, whom I came to know as Idris. I was the editor of the university's literary magazine and Idris came to me with some of his poems. We were all under the spell of Dylan Thomas, who had died four years earlier, and there seemed a special aura surrounding a Welsh poet which perhaps predisposed us to accepting the newcomer from Wales; but it was soon clear that young Idris had a voice of his own and was richly talented. We went our separate way when I graduated in 1959, and fifty years later, we are in electronic contact, he in Wales and I in Texas, and though physically a good five thousand miles apart there is beauty in the resumption of a spiritual friendship. I was happy to receive his new poems, not having seen his work since his 1970 book, *Barry Island and Other Poems*.

One important characteristic that has remained consistent in Idris's work is the freshness of imagery with which it is imbued; especially when his eye observes nature, his representation of what's experienced by the senses is often a new perception which is received by the reader as compellingly true—Pope's dictum of what oft was thought but ne'er so well expressed neatly describes Idris's imagistic observations. That is his poetical strength, what makes his poems a delight to read.

This may be seen in his poem 'Pavarotti in Llangollen' in which a vivid image sets the scene in the opening stanza:

> The hammock valley holds us into ourselves,
> green-walled, high horizons,
> in memory where music lies ingrained
> in the sway of grass and whisper of leaves.

The language seems direct, natural; but one notices the 'hammock' and 'music lies ingrained': the geographical picture contains within it the unexpressed idea of people, resting from their labour. People come to be within nature, which is composed of unheard music (reminding one of Keats's unheard melodies)—music with its associated idea of the harmony of the universe. The second stanza pans across the scene, showing scattered humanity, with the details about a young man climbing a tree and the son who wanders off and reappears adding a pointillist's particular dots to the general impressionist picture which stops with the eye seeing the painted long-boats in the water. Again very direct and natural, the language seemingly informal, and yet very suggestive. Then the one line,

> The orchestra played

takes one's attention to another direction, away from the scene of a rowdy humanity enjoying itself in primeval nature and into the mystery of the interior self, overwhelmed by music into silence. Then this wonderfully inspired image:

> It was the silence of many cathedrals
> split with sound.

It is heavenly music charged with divinity, a voice that enters one's soul and we are 'taken beyond mortality'.

In another poem, 'Green Country, Clwyd', there is one developing image presented in twelve vivid lines in which even an abstract remark—'Everywhere / there are fragments'—suggests there is something to be *seen*, making the whole poem a felt experience which intuitively releases the poem's central idea in the reader's imagination. The line, 'In the snow the smallest creatures leave their prints', lights up suddenly in one's brain and there's an explosion of meaning. This is pure poetry, natural, simple and yet pulsing with unexpressed, but profound, meaning.

An imaginative rendering that converts a modern political horror, such as Guernica, into a work of art produces a problematic poetry because the reader is predisposed to agree with the poet's emotional response. Examples where poets have succeeded are rare—Yeats's 'Easter, 1916' and Nuala Ní Dhomhnaill's poem on Srebrenica, 'Black', are two powerful successes that come to mind; Idris takes up the challenge with 'Treblinka', a poem written as a simple narrative in a matter-of-fact informal speech, and elicits a very moving response from the reader.

'Urology Ward', a moving poem about personal pain, well exemplifies Idris's gift for hitting upon startling and fresh images. In the poem's first stanza an old man in the hospital ward is heard to make

> a deep throaty sound
> like that of the wheels of a steam-roller
> pressing against chippings of granite.

This brilliantly captures the heavy weight of the human struggle against the tiny fragments of pain to which the body has been reduced and captures, too, the determination and resolve with which to attempt to crush the pain.

I admire an imagistic representation, even of nationalist subject matter—as in 'Iberian' where the argument of a nation's identity is made compelling in the image presented in the penultimate stanza:

> But, in the line of blood, we remained;
> a dark shadow on the cheek,
> the face an echo of the crescent moon,
> black hair, brown eyes and the
> blunt body, running to fat.

That 'blunt' is terrific. Idris reveals his talent for capturing the Welsh characteristics of people and things in some of his earlier poems (collected in *Barry Island and Other Poems*), such as 'Twilight, Ruthin', 'Hill Farmer', and 'Llandaff Cathedral', his eye always sharply focussed on some telling detail, his mind keenly inventing images which are charged with the poem's essential meaning. Indeed, I marvel at some of Idris's images—as in 'Gwndir' in which a killed rabbit is disembowelled and the poet sees the guts as 'white as porcelain, pale raspberry and smoky black', phrases of remarkable precision that create the impression that one is there looking at what the hunter has pulled out of the dead rabbit. Again, this is pure poetry, of which there is a good measure in this book to make it a pleasure to read and re-read.

Zulfikar Ghose
Emeritus Professor, University of Texas, Austin

To my wife, Denise,
on our 25th wedding anniversary

To my wife, Denise,
on our 25th wedding anniversary

Accord

In Memoriam, R.S.Thomas

It was not announced on the nine o'clock news.

In Pentrefelin, Twll-y-Cae remains,
its thick walls sheltering,
its oak furniture secure as history,
and, outside the gate, two metal dust-bins.

Dafydd y Garreg Wen lies in the old cemetery,
his song fastened to a hill over *Borth-y-gest*.
And Ioan Madog, my kinsman, lies under a marble pillar
– who wrote the hitting and lilt of *Port*'s once-schoonered quay.

He followed the bare hills,
as one of the faithful, fluently, through his pen.

He came into the dining-room
and when he entered, we all stood up,
Emyr, Kyffin, Matthew and I.

He handed out biscuits and talked
of the lanes of Arfon and Mon,
the stones, trees, birds, backwaters, quiet churches.

He brought us to the door,
his eyes and voice bright with humour,
mocking some churchgoer's manner.

He was brave.
He had hooked his face to the contraries,
placing his body in the wind and by the crooked trees
in man's mistrust and nature's non-forgiving.

As we left, he pointed to my car's name.
Accord, he said. *That's a good word.*

Green Country, Clwyd

Place is important on this globe
of furrows with troughs of memory
following our plough. Everywhere
there are fragments.
A mound of earth will make a stone, or Caesar.

The snow lies thick, hands-deep, worlds
lie in layers in one place. Look!
Look to the mountains anew.
In the snow the smallest creatures leave their prints.

Snow to water, dust to dust. But water
might be frost, or floods. Change ends in
change. Give everything a meaning, then
dirt is clay to the fist.

To Ioan Madog, Poet, Ancestor

Grandmother spoke of you
(as she lay, arthritic, in her bed)
as a large, happy man,
a blacksmith who shaped hoops for ships.
Porthmadog built them,
so many, you could dance from deck to deck,
the moil of labour in your ears mixed
with the rich note of the native tongue.

Nain died, and Grandfather
had seen before his death
the house he had built
over the water, near Port,
with a garden he laid for his lineage
– each stone he had carried
and the soil he had rubbed through his hands –
signed away, and later sold for profit.
The family, fallen apart, accommodated him
as distant harbours do a broken ship.

I have, my only remnant of the past's wreck,
a book of your *barddoniaeth*,
with Nain's writing beside the *in memoriams*,
telling of the dead, for me, in English.
And in the shaped and stormy lines
a couplet, once famous, lies in state,
its echo in the chapels failing now.

Gwaed y groes a gwyd y graith
Na welir moni eilwaith.

Although I speak a bastard Welsh
these words of yours, ancestor,
with their raging sadness,
might be a foreign tongue
whose cadence I know
but cannot translate.

Beside the estuary on a cold slope
close to their former home
my grandparents lie buried.
The cost of the gravestone was finally shared.
One day I looked for Taid's grave
but no stone then announced it.
Having failed, I stood in the long grass,
looked through the trees and over the choppy water
to the town famous for sea-captains
and the legend of Madog
who sailed, before Columbus, for the New World.

In Port, proud ships point no more
their carved bows towards distant seas.
A boat steams in occasionally
with raw materials for the explosives works.
The weekend sailing-boats are slim and haughty.
The wood has rotted, the mud has won,
and dogs roam the abandoned quays.
Port is bilingual, entertains tourists,
and on Sundays the young play tennis in the park.

The rich note fades:
The chapels loom:
The dirge seeps through the graven masonry.

Ni cheir diwedd
Byth ar swn y delyn aur.

So much is falling to ruin.
Let us hope, merely,
Ioan Madog,
poet,
that time will leave us something of your song.

Lawrence, Kansas

There was a wooden house on the side of a hill
in Kansas, right next to the University.
The woman there was barely over twenty,
had married at fourteen,
borne two children, divorced,
and was now with her second husband
of six months who wore an open-neck red shirt
and had just come back from the Pacific islands
where he had studied small marine animals.
He had maps of wide seas on his walls.

The girl in that house
cared for her children as if it was
not really her business.
And when she stacked up the soup bowls
she asked me whether I'd write her sometime.
But I have not written,
not knowing what to say to that figure
who did not believe in marriage and had only
gotten married again for the sake of the children.

After they had used the telephone
a young man appeared who was said to have no money
yet took courses in everything.
He had been at the university for a long time.
He sat on the floor beside me and the three of us
talked of how out in the Pacific
we would sail a boat
from island to island collecting copra
for there was plenty of it
and come back later with all that money.

When finally we left, the three of them waved to us
and I drove the Ford Mustang
smartly away from that house
and moved the car through the university on the hill –
the gear-shift snuggled in my left hand
with the bar across the palm and the chrome button
pressed with the thumb.
Then out of the town behind the car's long nose
and very fast on the thruway back to KC;
and I knew of course that with that yellow-haired girl
sitting quietly next to me
we were all like Mr Ford manufacturers of dreams.

As Beautiful as Architecture

As beautiful as architecture:
But architecture is *only* beautiful.

Cities that rise sweetly out of plains
are only playthings of the mind.
They do not grow as a man does;
they are not rubbed-down by generations.

Clwyd Street curves around your hip
as you walk down it.
Raise your hand – you can almost touch the rooftops!

It was from towns such as these
that Elizabethan sailors drew their pride
and sailed to the New World.

Brinley's new garage,
Will Bach the Butcher, Maldwyn J & P,
Capel Tabernacl, the Picture House,
Gwen's shop,
Crown House, the two Miss Williams's,
Capel Pendref,
The Square.

Architecture. Beauty. Yes, but
no man can plan a town.

Mister Clock, King of Polk Street

U.J.Clock, Esq.,
R.E.A. Inc.,
418 West Polk St.,
Chicago,
Ill.,
U.S.A.
was what I wrote
on the Air Mail envelope
I just posted.

I gave you an
Esquire.
I know you are
a man of
many parts.

Post Office building
with a hole in it
to drive through,
and you
in its shadow
drinking coffee
and smilin'.

Two large secretaries,
touching their hair,
reading the *Daily News*
are queens
in your Kingdom
of stained desks,
curly paper,
and that smile
I see now
coming out of the side of your face.

New Places

I once knew a girl
who borrowed the colour of the sun
as it stroked the hills of home;
who took the winds that pushed
the heads of trees in meadows;
who from her mouth, close-formed,
surrounded the whisper of the long river.

A girl who in the city
sang new songs
and suffered her mind to understand Humanity.

I knew her truth
as that of a tree lightly touched
by lightning.
And my truth, as wilful
as a sapling on the mountainside.

The winds and rains of ocean and hill
were used between us
and we fell apart
watered by new places and people.

And now I say, over and over again,
each has to grow in his own place.

First Day

I am teaching again.

Sitting on the edge of the table
I turn on the old tricks
like a performing animal.

They call me *Sir*,
go out and fetch me chalk,
and I hardly recognise myself.

Lunch-time, the talk in the staffroom
I recognise from past years,
old attitudes, jokes, introductions.
Then I wander out into the sunlight
where the boys play ball
and the sun glares off the tarmac.

A teacher besides me talks –
a small man with a sunken head
wearing an over-sized sports jacket.
He has applied for a job at ICI
after thirty years of teaching.

He doesn't like this school either.

Please God do not leave chalk in my pockets too long.

Aberfan

The word is written across the top of my mind
in thick black letters.
It has become public property.

When the black piper called the tune
and smothered those young faces
sitting in the beginning of the day,
orderly in their desks, then
after the frantic and hopeless clawing
of the elders at the murderous slurry, now
all we have is a name
claw-like and terrible, in black.

There was of course no time for panic –
they were snuffed out in split seconds
as efficiently as in a nuclear blast.

The Queen visited the scene.
The cold funeral with its cross of wreaths
laid out across the floor of the valley
came to us by courtesy of film and television.

The magazines received a flood of verse to mark the spot.
The customary fund for relatives was set up
and money poured in.
Toys piled up in the railway station.
Perhaps the grieving parents can forgive such mockeries.

That Friday I was in London.
We went to a bookshop on Charing Cross Road
where in the dark lower rooms
three Welshmen stood by the wireless
listening to the news from Wales.
They had known all this before.
Their shelves were full of memorials.

Later, driving to work,
the flags were at half-mast;
and, I thought,
that is fitting.

Few things are fitting
except silence.

Barry Island

Between the Haunted House,
the sea-blue wall of the Big Dipper,
the fruit machines, the trinket stall,
and the sea,

going round and round,
its horses on poles ascending and descending,
yellow and red,
words circulating around its roof
reading:

Here are
the ever popular
stand of galloping
horses and flying birds
patronised and enjoyed
by all classes.

Stand, circulating,
poised, clear –
all classes –
that's it, that's it,
that's how life should be.

Webster Street Junior School, Treharris

The quietness is alive.

If you put out your hand
you can feel their souls rustling against it.

They listen intently,
raise their arms, and look
with guarded wonder at the careful facts.

They settle down to work.

Pencils move vertically
in front of their intent faces.

The tall window is grey.
The Merthyr hills have been blurred all day.

Here,
  now,
    enclosed in a sense of love
    we are in eternity.

East Dock, Cardiff

This slab of water is no longer part of the sea.
It is still.
It leans against the quay with blue oil on its face.

Across the dock there is a ship.
It is as if in a dream we had put that boat there.
There are no seagulls.

The railway lines are rusty and lead nowhere.

Three warehouses turn their grey bulk to the sky
and let the weeds grow on them.

It is very quiet.

And yet we are so close to the centre of the city.

Bleddyn Griffith, Headmaster

I recall his voice,
his wide smile,
and the way when he turned a corner
the corridor became smaller.

He was not an educationist;
he would not solemnise the moment
for the lost cause of the universal.

He loved History and birds:
he watched them through long binoculars
merely to see them perform.

He shouted at us in the classroom
but we took little notice.
he left our souls alone.

Now, amazingly, the tall alive man is dead.

Sir, we your pupils –
for man is greater than he knows –
have you in mind
and say Thanks.

Elvis Presley

Truck driver,
found dead in his bathroom by an aide
then buried in a mausoleum.

Truck driver,
his father a cotton worker.
A raw boy from the south,
the rhythms of interlaced thruways and black night sounds
beating into his body.

There is a power which bubbles out of the earth
which was in his voice.
He could roar and whisper in the space of a second.

His voice was all that lived.
His body was a puppet.

His father kept his books
describing his crazy wealth.
He had no tax accountant, no investments.
The simple boy had it all as cash in the bank
and a fleet of Cadillacs and other toys.

Truck driver
with a voice like a twister
and a body owned by millions,
with too much money and too many fears.

And he died,
The King,
when his ordinary heart lost its beat.

Laugharne Castle

Against the cliff
like curtains
left after a play,
brown as mud, holed, ivied, roofless,
a straggled jetsam.

Between the houses of
Richard Hughes and Dylan Thomas,
surviving despite weather and neglect;
without improvement or attention or adulation,
it writes is own history.

Curlews call,
shoulders of mud glisten;
the sea swings, takes, changes,
moving sand, river and shore.

The castle remains
against the rocking and ooze of tides:
an eye and a hand
watching,
representing.

Concorde

Silver bird
rising from the runway
in a shimmer of heat and kerosene.

A picture of nature and man
joined and broken by nature and man.

The concord between
is a line of intention
sleekly drawn on the graph of the mind.

It makes no sense.
It is too sweet a machine.
It flies, it becomes,
it stretches in the air;
it is almost the air itself.

In the stratosphere it hangs
in timeless space, at *Mach* 2.

It is almost perfection
but, being man-made, it is not.
The concord is not complete.
The equation of man and nature
is not pure and simple.

Were it perfect, it would be –
like two panes of glass
held perfectly to the sun –
practically invisible.

Tom Pryce

In the pits in Silverstone –
wearing white driving overalls
and soft lace-up boots –
he stepped down from his changing-room in the trailer,
delicately,
like an astronaut.

He was surprisingly tall.

His friends were his mechanics, and his *Shadow Ford*.
(What was genuine was where the nuts and bolts were).

He was entranced
by the rigour of motor racing.

He died on the straight at Kyalami
through no fault of his own –
hit on the head by a fire extinguisher.

A freak accident; *out of the blue.*

A formal tragedy.

Now Ruthin mourns its hero,
his parents their son,
his wife, her husband.

You push yourself and the car
as far as it will go;
to the edge;
they know what it means.
Thus you fulfil yourself.

That, at least, is some consolation.

13th January 1993

My friend is buried today.

There is patter of rain on the window
and sounds of football played in the middle-distance.

Timed events surround me.
Light shines in the fading afternoon.

He was a cricketer once.
I saw him on an English green
near Cambridge, cap and flannel shirt,
performing the rituals of the secure.

He made buildings, but no life for himself.
He took his lack of luck badly.
His buildings had force,
thick wood, tall space, a place to live
and create and be.

But his being left him.
He had *What is the point?*
at the front of his mouth.

I remember a young man, fit
and confident, stripped to the waist in the rain.

I do not want to know how his body was
at the end.

National Eisteddfod

The Bard is crowned.
Horns shout.
A man gets to his feet in a pool
of admiring light.

The Archdruid asks, *Y gwir yn erbyn y byd;*
a oes heddwch?
The audience chants its reply
Peace.

It is lies. The truth is
part of the world, not against it,
or it is nothing.

In the real world now
small nations – Serbs, Croats, Muslims –
are slaughtering one another.

In Porthmadog tourists thicken the pavements.

The chip shop in Snowdon Street is busy.

Its young servers speak
inaccurately
the Welsh they learned on the streets.

Anglo-Welsh

To find a connection
between the hand holding the plug and the
  socket to receive it.
What is instinctual is what we know;
fitting the act between the cause and the conclusion;
  imperative; the mind's arrow
  and the muscled effect.

One morning, usual except for a detour,
on the road approaching Llandegla
from the Corwen direction,
I saw a round hill, white with morning frost
covered in lumps.
Dafad said my mind, unusually
forming a Welsh word
(for which I had no English equivalent)
in a leap to consciousness as a salmon throws
its lithe bulk to the sky.
The hill remained, a raw phenomenon,
as a shape out of my past
when Welsh was all my mind knew;
when sons of farmers came to school
their thick hands covered with warts.

And, days later, looking through a window
in a bungalow, a creature –
a grey rat-like shape with a tail –
leaped-up, stopped, moved again,
floated, edged, rose and ferried itself across the fence.
I was fixed.
Wiwer said my mind,
out of my past, when tall trees by the doctor's house
tousled their families of squirrels.

I stood dumb before the window,
stuck in the space between the past
and the present,
unable to translate.

Deeper levels in me than I know
speak Welsh to themselves.

I am perfectly at home in English.
But at times the eyes and the mind
fall apart, and I am left dumb,
holding the wire and finding
no connection.

Pavarotti in Llangollen

The hammock valley holds us into ourselves,
green-walled, high horizons,
in memory where music lies ingrained
in the sway of grass and whisper of leaves.

On the canal bank we chatted
with a man from Aldershot and a couple from Germany.
Picnic groups were noisy in the car park.
A young man climbed a tree.
Our son William wandered off and reappeared.
Painted long-boats
drew to a stop in the water.

The orchestra played.

Then on the screen, through the leaves,
above the white shirt,
appeared that whiskered face.

At the first note, the picnickers fell silent.
The young man froze in the tree.
Our son sat quite still.
The tree-trunks, canal and boats were as if
smothered in a brown amber.

It was the silence of many cathedrals
split with sound.
From somewhere quite different, that voice
came to us, each one.

Thank you. Thank you, he said between songs.
But the thanks were for the gift,
tangible (we were there, and he) but unreal.
From no everyday source
we were taken beyond mortality.

At midnight we saw him leaving;
a smiling face in a black car.

The Sampler

Fifteen years ago, in a junk shop in Caernarfon,
I saw on the floor a picture with a black frame
And a touch of gold, like a bible.
It was actually a sampler:
green lettering carefully hand-sewn,
flowers on cream cloth,
its layout deliberate and clear.

It read:
> *Er serchus Gof Am Ann Ellen*
> *Annwyl Briod Richard Jones, Syniet Terr*
> *Minffordd a fu farw Mehefin 6, 1901, yn 32 oed*
> *Ac a gladdwyd yn Mynwent NAZARETH*

It was bought.
And much later – because my wife liked it –
it was hung above the fireplace in our sitting-room.

Recently,
searching for family graves,
I walked up to Nazareth, Penrhyndeudraeth.
The chapel stands solid in granite, pillars, pediment,
looking over the valley where my mother
caught the *tren bach* to school;
Where Taid had his shop and where my parents were married
in a chapel now demolished.

In the lower graveyard, in a corner to the left,
I found my great-grandparents' grave –
Salmon Owen, Boston Lodge
Margaret Owen, Boston Lodge.

And looking slightly to the right
A familiar name rose off the gravestone –
ANN ELLEN.

Underneath, I read:
> *Anwyl briod Richard Jones*
> *Syniet Terrace, Minffordd.*
> *Bu farw Mehefin 6ed 1901*
> *Yn 32 oed*

It was the person in our sampler.
A co-incidence.
But who knows where and when the web of significance
will stretch and join?

In St. Mary's Church, below,
My uncle, John Williams, railway engineer, is buried
With *PEIRIANFARDD* after his name –
'Poet of the Machine'.

William, Richard, John, Margaret, Eleanor, Elizabeth.
Their names run in my blood.

The sampler hangs above our fireplace.

An element of immortality, deliberately made,
left, perhaps to be found
in a future
indifferent
except for my small reciprocal glow in the enormous dark.

A Field in Denbigh

Grass, thick and green, and cowpats,
with the hills behind; a triangular field
narrowing to a gate hardly wide enough to admit
a circus.

We waited. William played.
I had promised we would see them setting it up.
He kicked a ball with two girls from the circus;
one held his hand.

Through the corner came a caravan, then another, and soon
the field was spread with the makings of a circus,
controlled by a midget waving his imperious arms.
A Turk with a cummerbund spoke into a mobile phone.

Mrs Gandey handed out tea in mugs.
She spoke of the animal rights protesters – the 'antis'.
The midget came up, covered in mud,
and held his tea with a strong hand.

If it's too sunny they'll go to the beach.
That's no good for us, she said as the sun streamed.
She had white hair and moved well.

The water wagon came; the sawdust van;
the Ringmaster's mobile home in gold and silver.
A long trailer swung in to the centre,
the Big Top folded on it,
its shiny blue fabric with red stars, rather dirty.

We went to the afternoon show the next day.
Horses lounged around the ring, a girl slung;
a man in a small band blew his trumpet very hard;
long, fat, pythons nosed through the sawdust
and camels with two humps bowed their delicate knees.

During the interval, my wife said,
It's not very good is it?

In the second half, the trapeze swung and glinted.
Romanians leaped and landed – and not landed –
on one another's shoulders.
Beautiful black horses from Holland, plumed,
waltzed with three zebras.

At the gate, looking back at the tent and trailers
and the three elephants standing peacefully
in their roped enclosure,
it was a picture.

And now, the field is back again:
strong grass, the tall hedge,
the backdrop of hills.

We will forget our failures;
they are the currency of trying:
the setting-up, the anticipation, completion.

And William will perhaps remember
some small insignificant detail
like a broken cow-pat
or the blue ball he kicked.

My Love

after Roethke

I know a woman, lovely in her bones,
Who takes my life as on a cloud,

Who takes my weight and lightens it
And takes my breath to ease around herself.

I know a woman, lovely in her bones
Who, when she smiles, the earth smiles back at her;

Who leaves no shadow in the half-sun day
And spins the clock to end a cheerful week.

I know a woman, lovely in her bones
Who is the guardian of our being,

Who sings the song that binds us
And leaves each day a better time to be.

I know a woman, lovely in her bones
Who shares a fate and flesh with me

Who gives, unknown, a different kind of state
And takes my love with easy discipline.

I know a woman, lovely in her bones
Who answers not a single mystery;

It baffles me how mind and body knit
A garment of such binding constancy.

I know a woman, lovely in her bones
Who till my death shall stay upon my soul.

A Grave in Deia

We drove north from San Telmo,
the sea far below, through trees and scrub,
the road switchbacking.
Finally, tired with turning this way and that
we fell into Deia like an exhausted bird.

Out of the emptiness of the hills,
this was a jewel.
Centred between cliffs,
the church-topped village in shades of brown
was as if modelled in clay.

It is a place for egoists.
Your self comes back to you from the hills, magnified.
A place for making the self, and of the self.

In this eyrie in the hills
he – Graves – had displayed his fine head,
his plumage, his charm, his syntax.

We walked the narrow lanes and looked for his grave.
Around the church were laid
members of local families, photographs,
all in well-tended memory.
Fresh gladioli were laid on names carved in marble.

And then I found it, flat on the ground, a brown
rectangle of terracotta.
Written across its surface:
Robert Graves 1895-1990 Poeta.
That was all.

This brown stone, easily trodden-on and
not easily found, with its crude inscription
had not even the resilience of a paving-stone.

I thought of his reputation.
His name in all the encyclopaedias of modern writers.

Of the muse.
Of the women he had praised in lucid verse.

Not perhaps a pauper's grave
but the grave of one seemingly not part of the place,
its politics, history, religion, family-life.
His honour not dug into this earth.

In the distance, the Mediterranean;
a movement that in his youth
echoed the pulse in his veins
near Harlech, over Cardigan Bay,
seen also from a twisted road
between trees, above remote coves.

And I thought of my ancestor Ioan Madog,
celebrated with a column of brown Italian marble
inscribed with his poetry
in the old church of Pentrefelin.
He never had his name in *The Times Literary Supplement*,
but at The Ship pub in Porthmadog the barmaid told me
that (over a hundred years ago) he used to
write his lines in the front room.

And of Dylan – of the marvellous lyric –
under the white cross in Laugharne.
The locals speak of him, including his faults,
as one of their own.

In Westminster Abbey
there is a stone with Graves's name on it;
finely chiselled; beautifully made;
hard, cold, and alien.

David Lloyd

The name is enough
for those of us who remember.

A certain sound in the air
like no other.

His voice was like sweet rolling water.

Such ease! Such purity!
Such is Art.
Beauty stamped on personality,
alone, rare, unique.

He stood by the piano in our house
in Llanrhaiadr-ym-Mochnant – a local concert that night.
He had to practise.

A portly man in a dark suit with a waistcoat,
like a tax collector.
I could see the stains on his lapel.

And from the front room
the sound filled the house.

His voice was like sweet rolling water.

Palma Windmills

Motoring from the airport,
we see windmills in the fields,
winged finely like insects.
A message left by the past,
when weeds were dragged by hand from the soil,
when channels were dug and water pumped
by sails drawing the wind
in circles of hope.

A tower with lacery
as on the necks of Spanish women
who toiled, then rested on the Sabbath
drawing on their best clothes
in custom and respect.

Now the fields yield supermarkets
and block of flats.

Building, building;
the profit-makers
move their fingers over towers
of numbers, one on top of the other.

The residences of temporariness
pile up like ledgers.

On our way back to the airport
we flatter the driver.
We remember when this airport
was just a few rooms –
now, it is a fine place, we say.

It takes us twenty minutes to walk the corridors
to gate 35.

Cae Daniel, Rhos

Daniel, the farmer, lived in a tall Ruabon-brick house,
the master of his acres.
Now, his farm is only housing development
and a huge graveyard.

The dead sleep under tree and sky
with a long view towards Cheshire.
Fresh flowers are brought daily,
testimony to thanks and continuity.

Now the mourners enter
turning towards the fresh hole.
The young minister speaks clearly,
Sally is lowered, the rope hooks shaken free.

Uncle Jimmy is given earth in a plastic bag.
He steps forward, aged eighty-seven,
his mottled, shrunken face under a green trilby.

At the foot of the grave, he raises his arm,
palm upward, like an angel's wing
and from it, earth spills into the grave
as the best Mediterranean sand.

Pine Top's Boogie Woogie

with acknowledgements and thanks to Paul Oliver

Troy, Alabama,
birthplace, workplace.

1924
Clarence Pine Top Smith with Cow Cow Davenport.

Put yourself in Chicago.
in those boogie parties.
You go play
Boogie Woogie.

With Sarah Horton Smith they took a room on South Parkway
where they raised a family.

1928. Shot dead in the Masonic Hall, Orleans Street.

Meade Lux and Albert Ammons took it forward.
That black-alone, piano-alone.

Cleo Brown and Romeo Nelson
tried it.

But something of the early blues died with him;
some lightness,
the right-hand flicking and trilling.

Left-hand drives, right-hand sings.

The right-hand reaching for what Pine Top could do
and our left, pumping with the body.

Left-hand drives, right-hand sings,
and out of it, the ghost of Clarence Smith.

Have You Ever Heard of Cooney Vaughn?

The sleeve-notes say it was a Monday –
20 July, 1936.
Hattiesburg, Mississippi.
They laid down four tracks.

Play it Cooney, the voice shouts –
one of the Roosevelt brothers.
There were just three
in the Mississippi Jook Band.

Roosevelt on guitar, Uaroy on tambourine,
and behind them, too far from the microphone,
that great talent out of Piney woods,
from the bars and lumber camps
with a reputation but no fame.

Have you ever heard of Cooney Vaughn?

Dangerous Woman and *Skippy Whippy*:
his legacy from Forest County
on the Leaf River.

Listen to that piano
driving, controlling, saying
This is what I can do.

He was never discovered by an enthusiast
seeking out the original blues.
He worked and played at home.

Sublime skill
with his two friends.
A force intact.

Those of us who live in the backwoods
may have our talents too,
and in the future, a hundred years on,
someone might be listening.

Have you ever heard of Cooney Vaughn?

Death of a Language

I have heard the language die
in the corridors of Welsh-language schools.

I have seen the sour faces of Welshmen
distorted by hate.

Mae'r iaith Gymraeg yn marw.

I have heard the spirit of culture
drowning in the populist tide.

I have seen minds close
around the letter of language.

Mae'r iaith Gymraeg yn marw.

I have heard the bell tolling
down the one-way cave of history.

I have seen failure,
felt a lifetime's disappointment
in a people, backward-looking, shrinking.

Mae'r iaith Gymraeg yn marw.

What remains?

From the stony fields of Pantglas;
from two voices with harp on a platform;
from the starting roar of a sports crowd

comes at times
a movement, a sound,

so unique, so moving,
so much counter to the tide,
that it is like being visited
very occasionally
by a bird of
rare
magnificence.

Senedd

After five hundred years
we have built our boat
and settled on shore.

Roofed with hope,
floored in certainty,
this is a tent to talk in.

Sinews, tubed, flow to the sky.
Veins reach to the ocean.

Set in the mirrored sun,
we hope we can bathe
in more than our own light.

Leonardo

with thanks and acknowledgements to Charles Nicholl

Born in a farmhouse
in the Spring of 1452,
a winged lion, crest of the da Vincis
carved on the façade.

In Vinci there are reed-beds by the river,
a patchwork of shaded houses and fields,
olive-groves, an old mill and brown hills.

The winged spirit of birds lived in him.

He learned his craft in Florence
By Brunelleschi's dome (never equalled).

He drew machines – ropes, pulleys,
iron wheels, all the fine detail of engineering.
He offered rich men new ways to win battles.

And yet
in his paintings
there is the subject and the seeing;
detail dissolved in meaning.

A transparency;
movement which is halted;
light which is not sunlight;
colour which is not shape.

The invisible, visible.

Mimosa

with acknowledgements and thanks to Simon Sebag Montefiore

Such is leadership.

The stamp, stamp of personality.

In the figure in the greatcoat on the balcony,
moustache and peaked cap,
raising his hand to the masses,
setting the benign smile.
Below, the tens of thousands, the ant-like,
wave and shout in love of their leader.

Stalin's favourite flower was mimosa.

He held court like a Tzar
in wood-lined rooms,
his men coming to him in fear,
to obey, enact, and to secure
for themselves a future
away from the peasantry, the sour soil,
the long cold days.

Bolsheviks! A name to wave
at the obeying masses.

He took to power as a flower to water.

A superiority raged in this man.
It drove him, night after night, to out-drink
Out-eat, out-stand his colleagues.

He believed in his own Beauty.
His own *rage to order.*

He extinguished by numbers.
Tens of thousands were eliminated
for the sake of symmetry, necessity,
from the belief that he himself
was the ultimate in worth.

The ghost of his term still lingers,
echoing in houses with fine views
specially built for his pleasure.

Tyrants control and kill.

The flowers of death are with us.

Stalin's favourite flower was mimosa.

Floors

Our neighbour died.

We had seen her, once in a while,
in the garden;
a stooped body
marking quietly one decade
after another.

In the house she had built for her retirement
with her husband, a farmer,
she moved hardly a stick of furniture
but kept the block floors polished, year after year,
until they changed colour from fawn to red.

Laid by quiet men in 1950
in their criss-cross form,
they were in our house too.

Recently, I found myself on my knees
cleaning our floors with detergent and steel-wool.
I completed two rooms.

They are now as they were in 1950,
clean, fawn-blonde.

We live anew on our floors –
capable of life;
not preserving, cleaning,
not quietly marking the time.
And being more than a stooping life
and a brief funeral.

Avalon, Mississippi

in memory of John Hurt

It was almost nothing,
just a name on a sign,
a few houses
a place almost gone from maps.

He lived in a shack by a dirt road,
working the Delta,
sharecropping, planting, picking,
labouring the earth.

But when his hands took the strings
his neighbours danced
as his tunes filled the air.

Poverty was his home.
Music was his mind.

Avalon, sweet Avalon,
You make my music sing.

Boys' Brigade

They came into Borth-y-gest
on a Summer's day.

Around the corner,
along the bay,
in rows of three abreast
marching in unison.

Blue uniforms, pill-box hats,
braided in gold,
sharp creases on their trousers.

They had their bugles raised from their lips.
The tune they blew
skimmed over the water and
seeped into the crevices of the hills.

And much later
on the Cornell campus
from my car
I saw a queue of young men
waiting to be drafted.

I saw no bugles.
Heard no patriotic sound.
No pride in marching.

Just young men in shirts and jeans
on a Summer's day.

Sunday School Picnic at Garreg yr Hwch

The Berwyn Mountains –
like giants on their sides –
cradle the field.

In a hole in the black turf
clear water flows in the spring.
The sky is quiet with distant birds.

Ladies from the village carry food in baskets,
bread from the mill, butter, jam,
loose tea in a tin.

An arm reaches into to the grass
and out comes the kettle,
magnificent in black –
the fine swoop of the handle,
the sharp beak of the spout.

We gather kindling, it catches fire,
and the kettle begins to serve us
as it has done before
with its own song.

Sandwiches are eaten.
We play in the long stalks of the bracken.
All is happy and clear and reliable.

Fire and water, the Elements,
all have their stage here,
and happiness comes, as before,
in an orderly shape.

And when Nature comes towards us
with her wide skirts and warm breath,
I recall the arm
reaching for the kettle
hidden in the long grass.

American words

As a boy, I was fascinated by their names –
Kentucky, Chattanooga,Wyoming,
Colorado,Tennessee, Minnesota,
which hit the ear from far away.
Places of grandeur, confidence, beauty, romance,
vigor.

As a man, with his certainties gone,
I stepped down from the bus
in the Mid-West at 1.45 in the morning.
The horizon circled around me
and the distant town – DeKalb, Illinois –
was a scrubby oasis of lights.

One other person alighted.

I stood there in the extreme
emptiness.

From head to toe,
the cold penetrated my skin.

Facing my future,
I had lost my past.

And with what vigour remained
I reached for my suitcase
and walked.

Passchendaele

How was I to know
– child, youth and man –
that this steady man
who occupied the space before me
was part of that
tableau of horror?

As the years turned into decades
he uttered the occasional word –
Le Touquet, Ypres, Pilkem Ridge –
before I finally realised
that his being alive was miraculous.

I have a belt – wide polished leather
with brass fittings –
and a photograph of a straight man in uniform,
(August 1917),
the badge of the Machine Gun Co. on his shoulder.

I had a father, a banker,
master of routine and order,
but he avoided driving in cities
where his hands with their upstanding veins
started to shake.

And I recall the sound he made
at two or three in the morning –
a scream – which hit the doors and
walls of our house.
It had gone before I fully awoke.

It has stayed with me,
that partial sound,
almost hidden, like war.

Gwndir

Army-trained,
he raised his long gun to his shoulder,
left leg forward, knees slightly bent,
bowing his head to the stock,
pointing at the fleeing rabbit.

A hit. I shouted with congratulation.
The retriever brought the carcass back,
laid it down, waiting for praise.

The pocket-knife came out,
the rabbit slit down the underside.
The hand went in and out came the guts,
falling on the grass,
white as porcelain, pale raspberry and smoky black.
A trophy.

The knife worked again –
a slit in the ligaments of the back legs,
string fastening the carcasses together.

My flensing is complete.
I no longer exult.

I have pity for the killed
and some sympathy for the killer.

Treblinka

I cannot erase it from the landscape
of my mind.

The long lines of eastern Poland,
the sour land,
the dark, dark, blanket of fir trees.

Half a day from Warsaw, by bus,
towards Russia,
dark, dark, to black,
until a voice, tinny and inhuman,
from the plain concrete gateway
told us the facts about the death camp.

Inside, we walked in line, heads bowed, silent,
on the raised earth with its human remains,
between the tall stone monuments
with their long numbers of that country's dead.

From the earth, I picked up a piece of bone.
In the hotel, later, I put it in the wastepaper basket.
It was not a souvenir.

But I cannot dispose of that space
in the forest and those numbers on stone.

Sibelius

From where comes the confidence that rolls into this man?

I. *Finlandia*
London Symphony Orchestra; Hickox; 1988

As the nineteenth century turns in to the twentieth,
                                           I look to the east…
    The growl, growl,
        every breath exhaling the certainties.

    I assert. I demand.
    I drum. I strike.

I hold the audience in thrall.
Here. Look at this.
I am reminding you of what is in us.
This is you. This is me.
This is our being.
You cannot escape this.

Our myths are our energy.

I believe we can succeed.

And after the effort,
the resting, the hymn.

I praise.

I thank the Spirits for their recognition.

This is my credo.

II. The Second Symphony

New York Philharmonic; Schippers; 1963

Three notes. Points of the triangle. Turn it
this way and that, it remains.

The frost on the floor of the wood melts,
rivulets running, hurrying,
under the canopy of branches;

leave it to sleep,
the rumble of preparation for day.

Breath swings this way and that.
The spirit of optimism heightens.
The giant shifts.

The waters run to the river.
Waves form, rise and fall.

Trumpets call the day open.
The melding, the closing together of light,
the breath of animals, the pumping of energy
from the earth.

And we shall celebrate, certainly, celebrate,
our life here.

We are part of the rhythmical system,
trumpets call, extend the moment.
The fluids flow through me; I reach;
I am given energy.
I belong in the air.
I am given space;
I fly over high peaks;
I turn;
I extend;

This is my place.

Certainties roll forward,
long notes,
rising and falling,
as the heart beats,
once, twice, three times.

III. The Fifth Symphony
Halle Orchestra; Barbirolli; 1966

The happy land, springtime,
small flowers blossom,
branches spring up;
we are fed in the sun.

Small animals emerge, look about,
leap, leap, happily,
repeat, turn.

The land awakens.

Each side and the other,
a momentum,
one, then the other,
the dialogue.

We keep going.
We keep going.

Allegro molto. Strings.
Exquisite.

Moments,
periods of happiness.
Swinging forward,
continuous,
as the pulse beats.

I raise my hand and I bring it down,
Once. Twice. Three times. Four times. Five times. Six times.

I am complete.

Prisoner of War camp,
Llanrhaeadr-ym-Mochnant

Sad men, behind wire,
at the bottom of our village
wearing the drab uniform of the defeated, captured.

We, the children of the village –
free, unconcerned with international matters –
skipped past them,
those distant, quiet, creatures.

One day, a small inmate came towards me,
talking in low murmurs,
but I knew no Italian.
He held out his hand.
I understood that and gave him a shilling.

Next time I saw him,
he held out his hand again
and in it was a black tube –
a flute, made from a bicycle pump.

I took it home, blew a few notes.
Kept it.

Some of those men stayed behind after the war,
working on local farms.
You saw them
in the shadow of barns and tractors.

And now, when I look at the edges of the Tanat Valley
I recall the working flute.

Louis Armstrong's Trumpet

for James

How can a virtuoso grow
out of the meanest of streets?

They called him –
Illegitimate black child.

With that wide grin and round eyes
he was one of many thrown aside,
stereotyped into oblivion.

The New Orleans Home for Colored Waifs
had him in their band.
He wore their uniform,
strutted out in style.

Ragtime; they gave it a word
but it was more than that.
It was an invention
that floated on the spirit of a people.

Joe 'King' Oliver was his mentor.
At Storeyville he grew into genius.

We hear him now, on our car radios,
hanging in the air --
such power, certainty, beauty of tone --
and as he folds into the music of his friends,
cuts in with perfect pitch,
and holds that long, long, high note
we hear that fluent conviction
of great art.

Easter Sunday, 2008

Iberian

I was here long before the Celts came
(those bastards with their long knives).

We came in our leather boats,
pushing and paddling northwards,
dipping into bays, sleeping on shore,
avoiding the high waves and winds,
coming to a place green like home.

The Dyfi and Mawddach took us in,
struggling men, dark and sweaty,
our women muscled, hair tied-up.
We pulled our boats up the sand,
looked for shelter,
made our way inland.

We found the fertile acres
and the curved valleys.
Here our tents smoked and our grain multiplied.

But we lost the fight.
The others came from the east
with their language like spit,
looking for a home, as we had done.

We were driven down, vanquished.
Our way was not their way.

But, in the line of blood, we remained;
a dark shadow on the cheek,
the face an echo of the crescent moon,
black hair, brown eyes and the
blunt body, running to fat.

We left no language
but we remain in the code of nature,
in the shadow of hills,
in the tint of the human frame.

Llan

I was born with a dying language in my mouth.

to a people confident in their speech,
rich in the vernacular of demand and supply,
free of dogma and the requirements
of policy.

Now, the chapels punctuate a failure,
their insides like abandoned museums,
their blank faces and closed doors
lifeless as statues.

The language is being killed by kindness.
A stiffening orthodoxy prevails.
The air is full of good intentions
and a sense of doom.

Now we have a people bloodless with care,
made void by deliberation,
vapid with goodwill.

Their celebrations are trinkets and dressing-up,
with prizes given for poems with words
taken from old dictionaries.

The crows cry over the Tanat.

The hills are reduced by gentility.

I think of those farmers, their rock-strewn acres,
under the *pistyll*, their brown skin creased,
their eyes set on survival.

I hear their voices: first strongly
then slowly fading.

Down by the church, in the aftermath of history,
are the remains of a large book,
beautifully made.

They rise with the wind,
fold into themselves
and disappear.

Urology ward

1

The old man in the corner bed
with the Jewish face and large glasses
slept mostly, but when he started to wake
there came from him a deep throaty sound
like that of the wheels of a steam-roller
pressing against chippings of granite.

It was the tone of objection, protest,
of a life located in dissatisfaction.

My wife, he announced. *She died of breast cancer,
but she never drank or smoked.
She was good.*

He looked up at the nurse.
Am I safe here? he asked.

Of course you're safe here, she replied.

2

You're on the mend.

The phrase came across the air of the ward
as if written on a long pennant
gently unfolding in the healing summer breeze.

3

The Registrar sat on my bed
as I explained the nature of my pain.
He touched my arm.
It's normal, he said.

It will have gone in a week's time.

I walked to the car with some confidence.

And he was right.

That link with others we need
when we walk to the future.

Tabernacle

Slipped away –

A congregation,
the blood-driven hands, faces,
looking to God.

The Minister –
(his children
in the suburbs
enjoying the fruits of the language.)

The building remains,
an echo, a shell merely
of the soul.

Slipped away –

The hymns dissolved,
the Lord's Prayer gone into memory.

A people's unity, suited,
faded to the colour of cloud.

Slipped away –

There are no protests
as the mouth closes,
the hands limp.

There is a faint echo
and a sigh.

Count Basie in Manchester

We did not know –
and there was so much that we did not know –
that this man who sat at the table before us
had made so much.

That night the band he led had made a sound
like something we had never heard before.

Perhaps, to try to name it, it was
like some modulated wind
entering a huge cavern, gracefully.

Your musicians,
How do you know when to bring them in? I asked.
He had those hooded eyes, replying,
They just bring them and they play them.

He picked up his glass.
It was large, heavy, beautifully cut.
He took in the bourbon.

He was tired.

We knew we were outside our territory.

As we drove back to Keele
we were shadowed by a portly man at the piano
picking out the notes,
still making the sound
that he with the Duke and others from 30's Kansas City
had brought to a fecund, blossomed, pulsing, grandeur.

Spider

The man who painted my chimneys
killed himself by his own hand
a few days later.

He had stood tall on the cat-ladder,
applied plaster and – arms wide –
applied two coats of masonry paint.

In my bathroom, the next day,
a huge black spider emerged
and retreated.

Now, each time I look,
the spider – arms extended –
sits on my chimney.

Other

The shadow
is where she is.

The hill's thigh doubles,
each side equal.

The river cuts through the meadow,
left, right, together.

The sun gives to the moon
in its slow waltz across the day.

One is an image of the other,
time returned.

Her profile is mine,
her breath
an echo.

Stan Getz

Fastened in the window of memory
And the recall of sound
The girl from Ipenema goes walking

In Northern Illinois where the sky is distant and the
Ground rolls away in centuries
Tall and lovely, the girl

In the huge sports building
The saxophone kept behind
The sad voice, Astrid's,
Improvising, wreathed around the melody.

I hear it from this distance now.
It is classified, evoked,
And at times is the only thing heard

In the constant gallery of the magnificent dead.

Pennsylvania

He stood next to me at the grocery store.

Still as a tree, his clothes clean, worn,
scrubbed against those rolling acres.

From his jeans he took a purse,
placed it across his left hand,
handling it as if holding
the udder of a young cow.

Carefully he took out the coins,
cents and dimes.

His pack under his right arm
he strode towards the door,
leaving something behind,
indelible.

Elegy for Jimmy Yancey

James Edward
Tell 'em about me.

What horror it was for you, on the vaudeville stage,
twirling, raising your knees, a child
performing, next to your brother and father on his guitar,
entertaining.

A shy man. The rhythm of baseball claimed him.
In the All Americans team he threw and ran,
taking a job as groundskeeper for the White Sox.
He never quit his day job.

But at nights when the rents were due
he took his friends away from fear
with his beating left hand,
his right hand talking.

He taught Albert and Meade Lux.
But Pete Johnson had it too,
where the fire of the mind flows
beyond the point of knowing.

When both hands, together and not together,
syncopate the brain and being takes over
in a wall of explosions, flashing
in control and unexpectedness.

It was a Command Performance before the King and Queen.
The footman brought forward the black man.
The minstrel did some dance and some sound.
The royal party clapped.

And it was '39 before you recorded,
long after your friends had their names on the radio
and on the record labels.
Now he was ready.

And in Carnegie Hall in '48 with Kid Ory
you showed how the art from Chicago should be played.
The heart of the South was with you:
You showed the suffering and skill of a people betrayed.

In September '51you finished.
How Long Blues and *Yancey Stomp* were behind you.

As on the '78,
time up,
marked with E flat.

James Edward,
tell 'em about me.

Border land

I was born in March
between the articulation of Shropshire
and the hard grammar of the Berwyn hills.

My birth room between a steep field –
where sheep gave birth –
and the swerve of the Rhaeadr.

Slowly the village emerged from the centuries
under a cloud of silence.
Farmers with sacks on their shoulders
sat in their carts, their horses nodding forwards.

Here in a room in the vicarage
a young man decoded the ancient languages of Arabia,
turning them to the people's tongue.

And, over the border, later, another William
had his First Folio published, which also
altered the vocabulary of thought.

In this dual stream, my mind was made,
and as I have two arms, eyes and ears,
so the duet of language plays on,
joined, harmonious,
as one.